Turquoise and Mahogany

Annette Corth

Turquoise and Mahogany
Copyright © 2008 by Annette Corth

All rights reserved. Printed in the United States of America. No part of this book shall be reproduced or transmitted in any form or by any means, electronic, mechanical, magnetic, photographic including photocopying, recording or by any information storage and retrieval system, without prior written permission of the publisher. No patent liability is assumed with respect to the use of the information contained herein. Although every precaution has been taken in the preparation of this book, the publisher and author assume no responsibility for errors or omissions. Neither is any liability assumed for damages resulting from the use of the information contained here.

Published by

6500 Clito Road
Statesboro, Georgia 30461 (U.S.A.)

ISBN: 1-585-35-176-8

Author's Comments

Similar to the contents of my first book, these poems vary in subject from love and death and playing with language to humor and family/autobiography. Some poems fall into more than one category and others are denizens of a potpourri category. I have sorted the poems into six general sections and listed the contents of each section in alphabetical order to facilitate the reader's path through the book.

Dedication

I am grateful to my family, friends, and teachers for their support and encouragement in producing this second book of poems. I especially wish to thank my cousin and fellow poet, Naomi Glucksman Levine, for her continued help and inspiration and Ellie Hall Minnis for her technical assistance.

I have no children and leave my writing and my painting as a legacy.

TABLE OF CONTENTS

I. Love

Alone Again 2
Aquamarine Stone 3
Domination 4
Lodestone 5
Love 6
Love Is 7
Love Poem, an Ode to the Sensual 8
Rendezvous 9
Sacrifice 10
Seventies 11
Tarot Talk 12
Turquoise and Mahogany 13
Venezia 14

II. Death/Philosophy

Advice for Our Age 16
Brooten, Minnesota 17
Elegies 18
Eloise Dormer Williams 19
Encounter at Noon 21
Epigraph 22
Fortune Cookies 23
Gone at Last 24
Insanity 25
Life Among the Dead 26
Not Either Or 27
Questions 28
Selected Postscripts 29
Spring Lament 30
The Stone 31
Time on My Hands 33

Window Washing 34

III. Language

All in One Dream 36
Alone 38
Annette Corth 39
Beware the Poet 40
Fashion Statement 41
Middle Muse 42
Muse and Poet 43
Naming Art 44
Nine of Nine 45
The Poet 46
The Reading 48
Reawakening 49
Sestinal Dreams 50
Triolet 52
Villainous Villanelle 53

IV. Potpourri

Arrival 56
Birth of the Finger Lakes 57
The Body 58
Brown 59
Les Canards a Trois 60
Daffodils 61
Dark Clouds 62
A Dream 63
Found Objects 64
Impenetrable Cold 65
Kamikaze Finch 66
Light Verse 67
Messages from Beyond 68
Oranges 70
Patio Dragon 71

Picture This Picture 72
Puppet Head 73
Purple 74
Runcible Tune 75
Salt 76
Sawdust 77
Silken Cats 78
Silver 79
Soccer Teams 80
Storm 81
Tai Chi 82
Tank Fish 84
Three Peonies 85
Twilight 86
Twilight at Senior Housing, Ithaca, NY 87
Uncoiled 88
Verily 89
What Happens in the Night 90

V. Humor

Baby Bruin 92
Baton 93
Bun in the Oven 94
Butter 95
Geriatric Vacation 96
Go, Goat, Go 97
Gold-Threaded Wide-Brimmed Hat 98
A Great Golden God 99
Group Therapy 100
Host 101
If I Could Transform the World 102
Laura Doubting 103
Lewis Carroll Weds Walt Whitman 104
Literary Idol 105
Loveless Museum Image 106
Miser 107

Mythology 108
Obesity 109
Pillage 110
Quite a Day 111
Retirement 112
Stone from Hell 113
What's New 114

VI. Autobiography/Family

Almost, Almost 116
Beloved Grandson 117
Clench 118
Closing Moment 119
Cutting Back 120
Dark Encounter 121
Dear Greg Lardner 122
Divorce 124
Doors 125
Dream Colors 126
Ecce Homo! 127
Elegy 128
Exchange 129
Floral Echo 130
The Garden 131
Guilt 132
Heat 133
Hypochondria 134
I Twirl a Mirror 135
Kosher 136
Listen to Your Body 137
Mason 138
My Atrial Fibrillation 139
Not Yet 140
Pop's House 141
Progeny 142
Psychotherapist 143

Tale of the Manx 144
The Thing About You Is 145
Two Realms 146
Uncertainty 147
Under My Influence 148
What a Dish! 149
What Matters 150
When I Wrote About 151
Who Was to Blame? 152

Acknowledgements

Some of the poems in this volume have appeared or will in the following publications:

New York State Newsletter (Taoist Tai Chi Society of the USA), *Jews., Knocking on the Silence: an Anthology of Poetry Inspired by the Finger Lakes, Longview News* (Ithaca, New York), *Pegasus Review, Journal of New Jersey Poets, Home Planet News, Thumbprints, California Quarterly, Senior Circle* (Tompkins County Senior Citizens Council, Inc., Ithaca, NY).

Cover artwork by the author.

I. LOVE

Alone Again

How many anniversaries have I celebrated alone?

Once more you wandered away in answer
to unnamed yearnings for unknown places.
I remain bound to this little house,
the anchor of our intermittent happiness.

I close my eyes, inhale the perfume
exuded by the blue-green pine grove,
the acrid smell of burning leaves.

With all my inner strength I call out to you
across mountains, fields and waters
to return to my side. I summon you
in the black of night, again in the glow of dawn,
from wherever you may find yourself.

I strive to enfold you once again
in my hungry arms. I rejoice
knowing you will always return
even as my tear-burnt eyes prepare
to mourn your next departure.

Aquamarine Stone

I hold a gorgeous piece of glass
scraped by sand, shaped by sea,
irregularly rectangular, smooth,
nice to hold, not too cold, somewhat old,
and apparent that it's transparent.
Not navy nor cobalt nor sapphire
but like glacial ice, a gentler hue,
reminiscent of your azure eyes.

Domination

Yes! Yes!
At last, on top.
Don't move.
I, in charge,
set the rhythm.

I touch, I tease,
I threaten, I thrust.
You lie there wordless,
frozen, fearful.

Power pulses my
frame with frenzy,
thrills me beyond
anything you can
think of doing.

Why have we waited so long?

Lodestone

After we parted I began to roam.
With no destination in mind, I followed
curved roads, trusted to my wits and
innate sense of yearning.

Everyone I met sighed deeply, frowned,
not knowing where to find love or help.
All sought vainly to learn how
they might endure their feckless lives.

Many nights I spent escaping snow and ice
in a world rigid, colorless, void of hope.
But then you called to me from afar,
became an unwavering lodestone.

I move toward you, but know I must leave again.
We stand close, hold hands, utter no words.
Inhaling your scent, memories awaken,
transport me to where we had loved.

The landscape beckons, draws me in,
I smell the fragrance of pine woods, the acrid
smoke of burning leaves, hear the sound of axe
on wood.
Once again life embraces me and I weep.

Love

Love surpasses by far being-in-love.
Love is freedom from breathless anxiety,
coiled-up tension, jittery lightheadedness,
foolish titters, trigger-happy tears.

Romance bubbles and evanesces.
Love endures.

Love Is . . .

Love is savoring the timbre of his voice.
Love is catching the flicker of his embarrassed grin.
Love is relief as the garage door heralds his return.
Love is laughing in amazement at simultaneous thoughts.
Love is mutual acceptance of irritating habits.
Love is elation upon locating him in a crowd.
Love is shared sense of what is humorous.
Love is cherishing similar values.
Love is awe at his vast knowledge.
Love is trust, comfort, companionship.
Love just is.

Love Poem, an Ode to the Sensual

Warm, soft, affectionate without limit,
grayish brown hair, sparkling eyes,
snuggles on sofa at television time,
dining companion, shares my bed
dispenses caresses, nose-to-nose kisses.
Dearest cat, I adore you.

Smooth, brown, hard yet delicate,
softens sweetly inside of me,
yields waves of ecstatic pleasure.
Exotic kisses impossible to resist,
enticing, addictive, heaven-sent.
Hershey milk chocolate, I love you.

Enfolds me in steamy embrace,
fondles my every part and crevice.
Froth of delight slithers from
breathless head to willing body,
intoxicating scent of lavender, roses.
I passionately adore hot showers.

Shivers of fulfillment tease
my nose, my tongue, my eyes.
Subtle warm tones of brown, tan,
white, and rose seduce the senses
as soy sauce, wasabi, and ginger
enhance my lust for sashimi.

Yes, see yon stooped and grizzled
figure, scruffy of beard and wild of hair,
grumpily impatient but steadfast,
true companion of decades,
Renaissance man. How fortunate
he's mine, that husband I love.

Rendezvous

Many hours she sat in her treehouse,
awaited him in the shadowed perch,
their choice of childhood meeting site,
defying suspicion by jealous spouses.
Three decades earlier, they played there,
planned to marry, parent a dozen or more.
Twilight's chill embraced her, but he did not.
She imagined an accident, illness, a
business delay.
At full dark, she crept away, awash in brine.

Sacrifice

Belly afire, brow aflame,
half-closed eyes serenely stare
into void. Transfixed in
stance of acceptance, she
anticipates imminent demise,
a charred offering to redeem
love for another woman.
Spiraling smoke surrounds,
solemnly consoles, swears
salvation without end.

Seventies

We are dying; it cannot be helped.
Every move, every plan echoes
our years, our arteries,
the cancer, slow but growing,
heart rhythm out of control.

Each morning we crawl out
of night's fitful slumber,
shuffle aside nocturnal mist,
unshackle stiffened joints,
cleanse beclouded minds,
and slowly face another day.

While blood pumps
and muscles move,
brain functions
and memory slogs on,
we live, create,
squabble and love.

Tarot Talk

1.
You knew I was but twenty-one
and said I meant the world
to you. You snake, you stripped
me of my robe, left
me teetering on a globe,
crying for vengeance,
my banner black, unfurled.

2.
You were greedy, sought my crown.
Smiling, you flaunted your treasure,
tempted my ace of swords.
My beak tore at your gown.
I flew into you for pleasure,
my long neck encircling yours.
You cry for vengeance.
I weep for love.

Turquoise and Mahogany

Aries and Libra, half a year apart,
he admired dark wood, teak, mahogany,
wore clothes of deep brown, gray, black,
preferred women in somber tones
like starless night, blackest coffee.
She, enamored of shades of turquoise—
echoes of tropic seas, blue-green eyes,
voluptuous jewels—loved polka dots
and bold paisley. He was at home
in seriously subtle stripes.

At his mother's 60th birthday party,
Aries brought his love to meet the folks.
Lady Libra chose a silk, spaghetti-strapped
gown flaunting a scalloped hemline
and a pattern of vivid bands of turquoise
paisley alternating with bold stripes
of orange-yellow-accented mahogany.

He was appalled. His mother loved it!

Venezia

The last time I saw Marco,
day arrived slate-blue, cloud-laden.
My every dream reflects
watery images of the city where
we met and loved. Desolate gondolas
bob, deserted, unpeopled. In murky
haze beyond our favorite bridge,
the phantom cathedral looms.
Peppermint mooring posts
lean at jaunty angles, emit
the only flicker of hope
of his return. I wait. I wait.

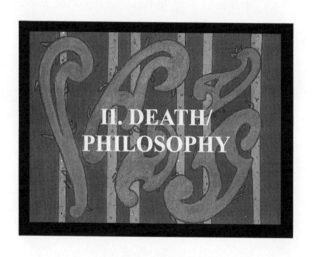

Advice for Our Age

Happiness, how delusional, unreal.
Discord alone has staying power.
Nations resort to rape, lies, torture.

Lives flounder in a flood
of fear and greed and pain.
Harmony is an illusion, a scrim

concealing loneliness, lost love,
betrayal, brute force, false hope,
incest, ethnic cleansing, corruption.

We can depend upon despair,
the darker the better. Forget trust.
No one is any damn good,

especially apostles of smiley faces,
singers of pious hymns,
and candidates for office.

Brooten, Minnesota

Daughters of Norwegian immigrants, we spent
our early years on the large dairy farm
just outside of Brooten, Minnesota.

Between chores we seven siblings all
attended the town's two-room schoolhouse,
felt ourselves comfortable, safe.

On December 8, 1912 a conflagration
decimated the core of our farming town,
the only home we had ever known.

Lost in flames and collapsing walls
were post office, general store and church
as well as grange, police station, our school.

The smoke cleared and heads were counted.
We had given unto the Lord's hands one grocery
clerk, the minister, the town nurse, all three
of my younger sisters.

Why these particular folks? How to explain the loss?
Foreordained, random whim of a malevolent deity
or merely inexplicable?

Elegies

Many died right there. We mourn them all.
Ribbons of tears down visages fall.
Music diminishes, birds seem mute.
Once a symphony, now a lone flute
serenades our lives, the loss acute,
each departure silencing a tone.
Like a skeleton bereft of bone
the body cannot exist alone
but droops in sorrow to weep and moan.

Eloise Dormer Williams

I was jealous of my little sister,
Felicity Rose. She was pale and
slight of figure and acted weak
and helpless. Folks, especially
Father, doted on her, made no secret
that she was the favorite daughter.
Because she tired easily, Mother
always gave her the least
strenuous chores.

For several years a neighbor,
young George Benton, courted her.
Our folks thought George a nice
enough fellow, clever and dependable,
and were pleased that after milking
his herd of dairy cows, he would
visit us and spend the evening
playing cards and telling the family
amusing stories.

When George asked for Felicity's hand,
he met with unexpected opposition.
Our folks felt she was too young
and too delicate to undertake
the role of wife and mother.
However Felicity and George
persisted and prevailed. Just shy
of her eighteenth birthday
they were married in the Baptist
church down in the village.

(Continued . . .)

Gentle George, loving and thoughtful,
treated Felicity like a flower.
Since they wanted to start a family
right away, she soon became pregnant.
Two weeks ago, after twenty hours
of labor, she presented him
with a lovely little girl. The happy
father gave his wife a cut-crystal vase
full of bright red roses and delicate
baby's breath, her favorite flowers.

Poor George. The vase of flowers
still stands by their bedside. The roses,
now deep maroon, huddle together,
dried out and curled back on themselves.
Their leaves and the baby's breath droop
on browned stalks. Water at the bottom
of the vase lies murky and fetid,
crowned with translucent lacy scum.

Now I am the family princess. Three
days after the birth of her daughter,
Felicity Rose Dormer Benton
left this world, felled by a
combination of difficult delivery
and acute consumption.

Encounter at Noon

The sun inched up the splintered
handle of his rusted blade
as the man crept toward the barn,
hearing the return of the intruder.
At noon the axe descended,
its thud eliciting a muffled
gasp followed by upward showers
of fur, wood chips, and blood.

Epigraph

I have suffered the atrocity of sunsets -
　　　Sylvia Plath in "Elm"

Why does your claim intrigue me so?
How syrup-like it glides off the tongue,
how enigmatic its image.
Tell me, did it convey a secret message,

didn't intend to, was a verbal teaser,
or was it an attempt to garner pity,
extract empathy from the puzzled reader?
Sylvia, how can a sunset be atrocious,

intrinsically evil, chromatically cruel?
The suffering, was it toleration or pain?

Perhaps sunsets were your code for despair,
eventual loss, hopelessness; or
were those words a parting blow,
a final cry to a worrisome world?

Fortune Cookies

Measure distance in hours not miles.
An old lover will cause you trouble.
Beward of your mother's ancient wiles.
Many a gem lies buried in rubble.

Is the artist or is the model posing?
Guilt and fear lurk in lonely minds.
All entrances foreshadow their closing.
Woo darkness when disclosure blinds.

Forgive an enemy with acts of grace.
Sorrow heals in moonlit streams.
Your fortune lies in a hidden place.
Follow the essence of your dreams.

Gone at Last

The geese in their migration southward
ignore with honking mirth her departure.
Neighbors relish freedom to rejoice
as clouds reveal the glow of solar gold.

The backyard flowers revel in her passing,
anticipate a gardener of greater skill.
No one cherishes her belongings, deep
in decrepitude, nor stoops to ponder
the self-centeredness of her life.

The hoary witch took her time to die.
As her grip on us loosened, the sound
of her carping complaints silenced.
We who knew her suppress recollection
of her century-long existence and take
delight in our new-found serenity.

May the old hag rest in hell.

Insanity

I hear 'em breathin', alien assassins
out ta get me. Voices whisperin' lies
on 9-1-1. Got me fired for stealin'
'n' abusin' customers. Lies, just
lots of crap. What's ta steal from
McDonald's? Insult a dump truck?
I ain't gonna put up with it no more.
Killers are stalkin' me disguised
as bag ladies 'n' seein'-eye dogs.
They put cameras in da urinals
in bars 'n' bowlin' alleys, made
dogs pee 'n' shit by my front door.
I'll git a gun; I'll blow 'em away
'fore they kin come 'n' waste me.

Life Among the Dead

Gelid mist obscures all vision.
Soundless ambience reveals no hint
of place or time, up or down.
Formless shapes appear then fade
and phantom murmurs seduce the ear.
A silent aura of pulsation
incessantly throbs like the beat
of music sans notes, suffuses
oblivion. There exist no thought,
no feeling, no memory—end without end.

Not Either Or

There is no really safe place,
no all-sheltering haven.
Life a constant source of fear,
loss of loved one, serious illness,
injury in accident, becoming lost,
ridicule by others,
Alzheimer's.

Countering ever-present fears
are occasional reassuring things,
clouds of birds about a feeder,
tender touch of a loving cat,
yielding to intoxication of chocolate,
intricacy of language,
love and praise from friends.

Questions

Were you ever enveloped in January's grasp
while Nordic skiing and gotten lost,
wondering whether you would ever be found,
and then rescued from the frigid forest frost?

What was she like, the woman you called mother?
Was she a princess, to the purple born?
Did she tend rather than love you?
Did she leave you cold, of her love lorn?

Have you ever had recurring dreams of isolation
with everyone else possessing a friend, a mate,
but you alone enfolded in profound panic
knowing lifelong aloneness will be your fate?

Is your own body betraying you,
filling you with loathing and fear,
forming lumps and growths and sores,
warning that mortality is near?

Who knows what abides in the ocean,
source of life for all creatures,
some of earth, others of sea or sky,
each with unique biotic features?

What dwells in the caves of winter,
sluggishly peering out into wild
and desolate, frozen land,
fiercely guarding its sleeping child?

What if there really is a God,
despite the failings of Her creation
and myriad broken promises,
who will grant us eternal elation?

Selected Postscripts

Here's one from 1929 from Uncle Joe,
the New York banker, who
appended an apologetic farewell note
to Aunt Mabel and their kids
just before his leap into space.

In 1943 my kid brother Ben,
a young marine in the South Pacific,
added a greeting to the letter written
to his unborn son, Jonathan, whom
he never lived to know.

A college student in 1962,
cousin Matthew begged
his parents for additional money
so he could secretly buy LSD,
which slowly killed him.

The last month in 2006 I sent
my grandson Dakota a request
on his birthday card to please see
that the book of my stories and poems
gets published after I'm gone.

Spring Lament

A drift of sadness deadens the scent of spring,
wills winter's return, defies renewal's dawn.

My eyes wince at vernal brightness, the rush
to emerge and sprout, replace brown with green.

I savor the shards of memory of meals I shared
with my friend, newly gone. Food now tastes of ash.

I miss the warmth of Harold's hand extended
with loving pressure, confirming our secret bond.

I hear his voice entwined in breeze and birdsong.
How dare spring come when he is lost in winter!

The Stone

Somewhere in northern New Jersey
a modest tombstone, its inscription
dirt-filled, barely legible, stands
crammed into an old Jewish cemetery
encircled by industrial plants and strip malls.
Beneath the granite resides Morris Rubinstein,
whose heart was burdened by a ponderous
stone. The stone's fissures traced the sadness
and disappointments of his long life.

The stone lodged in his heart even before
Morris, immigrant from a land of pogroms,
entered through Castle Garden in New York
Harbor. In Russia, someone had tricked him
into marriage to Jenny, sister of the woman
he loved. They produced five children, lost one
in infancy, never got along. He spoke
Yiddish, Russian, Polish, very broken
English. The difficulty of speaking
with his six grandchildren or the spouses
of his children laid granite in his heart.

The stone grew with his expanding girth.
His youngest granddaughter fled screaming
whenever the huge man approached.
At 65 his work in a fur processing plant
ended. A widower, self-isolating,
consoled by alcohol, his final days
became a pile of pebbles and shale.

(Continued . . .)

The old man attempted to be jovial, told clumsy jokes, tried to mask his profound unhappiness. His daughters treated him like Regan and Goneril, shuttled him between their homes. Morris left his life screaming as the heavy stone crushed his heart.

Time on My Hands

As he lies dying in his sweaty bed,
I have time on my hands.
I wander through colorless halls
to nearby waiting-room window,
watch hawk catch raven on the wing,
dislodge one bloodied black feather.
I have time on my hands.
Once more I go back to his sterile room,
looked at unseeing eyes, heaving chest,
slowly return to the waiting room.
I have time on my hands.

Window Washing

Vision of life streaked
with stains of friendship lost,
smudges of love forgotten,
pain remembered.

Surface of glass through
which I peer, soiled
with anger, jealousy, fear.

Overall film of dust and grit
imprisons. I seek the water
of hope, the cloth of courage,
soap of strength, to wash my windows.

III. LANGUAGE

All In One Dream

Memory, fantasy, hallucination   recurring, repeating, reiterating   fanciful, improbable, unreal   dark, sinister, brooding   in manner, mode, mood.

Water walls   advance, approach, attack   inundate, wash over, overwhelm   blanket, towel, shoes   on beach, shore, strand   dismay, frighten, terrify   mother and child, daughter and parent, Mom and me.

Then, thereafter, next   I wander, walk, roam through familiar, known, home   town, city, metropolis   seek alternative route, quicker path, direct way   to main avenue, central street, chief boulevard.

Encounter, meet, come upon   puzzling, unexplained, baffling   locked doors, dead end alleys, strange buildings.   Enter, pass through, invade   gardens, living rooms, kitchens   of bemused, surprised, annoyed   people, neighbors, strangers.

Dire, pressing, uncontrollable need   to find, discover, reach   restroom, "ladies," toilet   not subject to, stalked or harassed by   voyeurs, peeping toms, rapacious men—a facility free, unoccupied, private,   void of, lacking, without   unpleasant, vile, malodorous   status, condition, aura.

Guilt, reservation, fear of discovery   of loving, intimate, passionate relationship, feeling, attraction towards   attached, unknown, incestuous man.

Swimming, stroking, paddling   in large, spacious, outsized   pool, pond, lake sans anxiety, fright, fear of water.

Late, tardy, untimely arrival   for important, special, vital   meeting, class, appointment despite personal punctuality, innocence, lack of fault.

Writing, penning, composing   pretentious, ponderous, overwritten,   phrases, sentences, prose poems.

Alone

I roam and ponder lacy memories,
forgotten silken dreams and veiléd fears,
alone on icy textured mountain peaks,
I stand unclothed, afraid, awash in tears.

Annette Corth

In Ithaca did Annette Corth
A stately treasure-poem create,
Where our Cayuga floweth forth,
Not running westward but due north,
    Down to an icy fate.
There twice five stanzas did draw breath
With metaphors including joy and death,
Perfumed phrases blossomed into rhyme,
Every image sought its rhythmic mate,
Their meters blended into verse sublime,
Producing thoughts to contemplate.

Beware the Poet

The poet weaves a web of honeyed guile,
creates a Trojan horse upon each page,
proclaiming love but full of hidden bile.

She lures the reader with her subtle wile,
induces fits of tears and often rage.
The poet weaves a web of honeyed guile,

an ode to warmth, to friends, a gracious smile,
describes the glow of our joyous age,
proclaiming love but full of hidden bile.

Beneath the surface lurk her symbols vile,
their inner meaning clear but to a sage.
The poet weaves a web of honeyed guile,

misleads the reader by her polished style,
produces sorrow, anger, hard to gauge,
proclaiming love but full of hidden bile.

Her metaphors confound us (such a trial!).
In this manner writers earn their wage.
The poet weaves a web of honeyed guile,
proclaiming love for just a while.

Fashion Statement

In far away Frankfurt,
fashion fascinates fanatic
flashy Fascist females in
fancy full-flared flax and felt.
Striped skirts sewn with scarlet
swastikas on silken seams seduce
sexy stylish singers to swoon
over shaggy cerise satin socks.
Frilly fur frocks physically fit,
but for fat Fraeuleins, the Fuehrer
favors flimsy flowered flannel.

Middle Muse

Wearied of its diurnal journey,
the sun sighs and sinks its head
onto a mauve and orange pillow.
The wind holds its breath
and then drifts off. Birds nest
in silence in their secret spots.
The cat lies coiled around himself,
flicking his tail, dreaming of birds.

Now comes the ideal hour to pen a poem.
Begin at the start. Finish at the end.

No rules for me. I will sing unfettered,
choose the middle as the peerless
point from which to birth my words,
both forward and aft. Acorndownward,
my poem will spread as oak tree roots,
embracing the earth, and then rise
upward as trunk, branches and leaves
bestowing beauty, shelter, solace.

Muse and Poet

The poet faced her table, pens at hand,
The poet faced her table, pens at hand,
nearby a stack of paper, hungry for ink,
nearby a stack of paper, hungry for ink.
The hungry poet faced ink for her paper,
at hand, nearby table, a stack of pens.

She opted to muse about her muse,
She opted to muse about her muse,
disparate thoughts, random images,
disparate thoughts, random images.
Her muse opted, random thoughts,
she, to muse about disparate images.

Harmonious word combinations,
Harmonious word combinations,
capricious metaphors, feral rhythms,
capricious metaphors, feral rhythms.
Harmonious metaphors, feral combinations,
capricious word rhythms.

The feral muse faced random pens,
disparate paper, her table nearby.
Her stack of hungry metaphors, rhythms,
opted to muse about a capricious poet,
she, ink combinations in hand for
harmonious word images, thoughts.

Naming Art

We come upon a work of art
and seek to know its title.
Untitled, a slap in the face
by mean-spirited artists,
who disdain to reveal intent.

Did the artist contemplate
a tallish mountain, a smallish fountain,
a rather old donkey, a somewhat cold monkey,
a quite green flower, a very mean glower?

Tell us, artist, what did your muse portend?
Otherwise, you have lost us in the end.

Nine of Nine

Let form control content this one time,
determine metaphor, meter, rhyme.
Write a poem totaling eighty-one,
nine lines, nine syllables per. It's done
when filled with visions of moon and sun,
early love, silken cats, childhood dreams,
exotic landscapes, cold mountain streams,
computers, daffodils, laser beams,
elegies, nightingales, soccer teams.

The Poet

The poet faced her table, pen in hand,
nearby a stack of hungry paper eager
to eat ink. Poet began to muse about her muse,
disparate thoughts, random images,
harmonious word combinations,
capricious metaphors, feral rhythms

   such as

Music in crystal spoons encourages
small thoughts in expanding spaces.
Staplers unite with resonant finality
like trumpets and bells heralding alarm.

       or

Swim like an eagle,
fly like a cobra,
crawl like a tilapia,
run like an amoeba.

          also

Fallen leaves rid a tree
of the burden of bearing
them in wind, snow and hail.
Pine needles pierce, their
pungent aroma exhilarating.

            and

Animals are warmer than stones.
Cactus impales small creatures.
Mosaic minds lack luster in moonlight.
My grandfather was obese, alcoholic, always sad.

    now

Here is a plethora of grist to grind
into throbbing emotion, poetic song.
The poet will try with heart and mind
and birth images vivid and strong.

The Reading

The weight of one hundred poets
worries the load bearing
of a musty storefront floor.

Writers wait with bated
impatience for the poetic
reading meeting to commence.

Would-be poets crowd there,
shoulder to shoulder, butt to butt,
each upon a creaky folding chair,

row after row, jammed wall to wall,
winter coats taking space
from each derriere on its place.

Cumulated BTU's suffuse
the store with body heat, smell of sweat.
All the writers squirm and fret.

Then chosen readers rise to speak
(in standard monotonic voice)
their piece, pursued by murmurs

of applause and silent sighs.
One hundred minds without a sound
opine, "My poems are more profound."

Reawakening

A sentence starts out like a lone traveler
heading into a blizzard at midnight,
tilting into the wind, one arm shielding his face,
the tails of his thin coat flapping behind him.
    Billy Collins   "Winter Syntax"

Three months, no syllable written.
I push myself to energize a pen,
unleash words caged in malaise.
A sentence starts out like a lone traveler.

Then words emerge from clinging doldrums,
form phrases, reluctant sentences,
unclear of destination or purpose,
heading into a blizzard at midnight.

Decisions loom—serious or light?
A frame seeking a picture, I select a mood,
shades of emotion, but not description.
I *tilt into the wind, one arm shielding* my *face.*

My eyes cascade freely, my nose swells.
An eruption of feral feeling quakes me.
I rue the liberation of dormant pain
as tales of my past *flap behind* me.

Sestinal Dreams

I should not savor such a sordid scene—
spectral shadows, spiraled stars, sounds that soared
above and through a sodden seeping seine
that shimmered in the bloody, scarlet sun.
A sudden shift, a shredded sail in sight;
stiff winds screech, falter, begin to smart

as six sly satyrs scream and act too smart.
A shower of snakes saturates the scene
stalking skeletal sharks to the site
where sick swans shout and fall upon their sword.
Twin sailors on a spree seek out their son
somewhere southern and sublime; they seem
insane.

A serpent starts to stain the seine,
stimulating interest in some art
scribbled on sand by a sulky son
in sexual strokes, cerise, obscene.
A silver celebratory sword swathed
in silk, slays the son, sinks from sight.

The sadism of that which soon I'll cite
surely shall surprise. You doubt you're sane;
serenity shrinks, fears to have soared.
Sorties of stingers cause skin to smart,
tornadoes of scorpions sate the scene,
strangle your breath, suffocate the sun.

Seven cyclists swim in the scorching sun
singing saucy psalms: such a solemn sight.
Sous-chefs offer succor, a stirring scene,

to schools of salmon and a stork. Not sane,
so I say, but somehow sort of smart,
sinister shepherds start to swing a sword,

slashing seagulls that secretly have soared.
Some solution exists under the sun
to escape this dream and come out smart
enough to squelch the starkness of the site,
to slice asunder the said strangling seine.
Slumberer, arise, subdue the sorry scene!

The sword I cite,
swung by a son not sane,
will smart those on the scene.

Triolet

It sure looks easy, very safe to try.
I'll write a triolet, that gift from France,
mood and subject to appear by and by.
It sure looks easy, very safe to try.
If a failure, I'll mope, may weep or sigh.
If successful, I'll crow and start to dance.
It sure looks easy, very safe to try.
I'll write a triolet, that gift from France.

Villainous Villanelle,
Ode to a Calendar Picture

My June calendar features a saccharine bitch
Whose filmy garb and feeble wings would feign
The outward antithesis of an evil witch

She hovers among flowers, the epitome of kitsch
The sight of her gives me deep psychic pain
My June calendar features a saccharine bitch

The golden waves of her hair seem so rich
They strike me as completely inane
The outward antithesis of an evil witch

If I could, I'd dump her in a roadside ditch
Filled to brim from summer rain
My June calendar features a saccharine bitch

She endeavors to usurp a fairy tale niche
Through deception that is truly in vain
The outward antithesis of an evil witch

If it were in my power, I'd make her switch
Back to her cronelike self in the main
My June calendar features a saccharine bitch
The outward antithesis of an evil witch

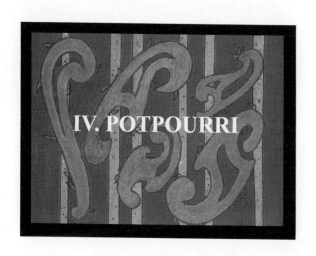
IV. POTPOURRI

Arrival

A faint tinkle, tuneless,
then a fuller steady throb
followed by coughing roar.
A male voice shouts,
announces, beckons.
Doors slam, children scream
and plead. Clink of metal
against metal accompanied
by laughter, murmurs of pleasure.
The Good Humor man arrives.

Birth of the Finger Lakes

Tens of thousands of years ago
the mile-high wall of ice slowly
loosened its grip on Earth.
Advancing arms clawed
vast stretches of landscape
leaving deep gouges behind,
finger traces of its ravages.
Earth warmed and the frigid mass,
reluctant in retreat, gifted the grooves
with tears of its diminished self.

The Body

Veins, arteries, bones, skin,
heart, liver, brain, intestines,
nails, hair, eyes, teeth,
blood, urine, feces, bile:
created from disparate cells,
returning to component
elements.

Shrine to house the soul,
container for spirit and mind,
begetter of depravity and lust,
adored object of beauty,
source of embarrassment and shame.
Wondrous mass of minerals and water,
triumph of DNA.

Brown

Chocolate, of course, but also excrement,
rich soil, scorched meat. Hue of undyed leather,
telephone poles, sun-tanned Caucasians, people
of African heritage. The color of bears,
beavers, moose, winter birds, burnt toast.
Earth tones—umber, sienna, sepia.
The nose of a toady, rosewood tables,
raisins, cinnamon, baked beans, molasses.
Jeannie's hair, my eyes, muddy water,
tincture of iodine, extract of vanilla, coffee.

Les Canards a Trois

April, bleak April.
Our pond, ice-rimmed,
monochrome, hunkers
down amid Holstein banks.
Emergent rocks mingle
with clumps of tired snow.
The pregnant sky bodes
another birth of precipitation,
unwanted.

First robins waddle by the pond,
as it hosts subtle splashes,
widening concentric rings.
Icons of constancy,
our ménage a trois, mallard
princess and petit entourage
of two male suitors,
returns for its vernal sojourn.

Daffodils

Jonquils, narcissi and daffodils,
cousins, fellow denizens of spring,
herald demise of snow and ice,
predictable, yet surprising
in vernal regularity, bulbs
burgeon through many winters,
spill over into flowering sea
with breakers of yellow, orange, white,
crests single, double, fringed.
Waves of delight.

Dark Clouds

Dark clouds hover over the churning lake.
The weather shifts from benign to mean,
Leaving torrential rain in its wake.

The gardener flees, forgetting her rake.
Drenched, cold, she escapes the worsening scene.
Dark clouds hover over the churning lake.

Nothing moves save a frustrated drake,
Attempting, despite the downpour, to preen,
Leaving torrential rain in its wake.

Drake and gardener an odd couple make,
United in fondness for calm and green.
Dark clouds hover over the churning lake.

The gardener's heart, lacking sun, does ache.
Clear skies and warmth for her would be so keen,
Leaving torrential rain in their wake.

I hope the sky would brighten for their sake,
Making duck and gardener feel serene.
Dark clouds hover over the churning lake,
Leaving torrential rain in their wake.

A Dream

I had a strange and wondrous dream
    of outer space and inner space
    of azure spheres and silvery floating veils
    of vague organic forms drifting by.

Imperceptibly the forms grew then exploded
    into vivid, soft-hued shapes,
    simultaneously cosmically enormous
    and infinitesimally small.

All constantly moved across, behind,
    over and through each other,
    elegant, harmoniously choreographed
    but approaching chaos.

Their unity was slowly destroyed
    as the spheres tore themselves
    from the dancing forms,
    their universe disintegrating.

In chaos the dream vanished,
    leaving my inner world in fragments.
    Now nothing remains but a fading particle
    of an imperfect memory.

Found Objects

White pottery shard, triangular,
half an inch thick, smoothed edges,
left in deserted rusted station wagon,
guarding knitted pale green infant's
cap, the cap partially unraveled,
stained with dried blood.
Moribund wagon abandoned
in shadow of railroad trestle,
chaperoned by household trash,
jumble of sentinel weeds.

Impenetrable Cold

Ponderous glaciers
suffocate and
lacerate the earth,
kidnap remnants
of distant river beds
and verdant valley floors,
erase all remembrance
of warmth and love-filled days.

Kamikaze Finch

Sudden thump against glass deck door
leaves finch lying on the wooden planks,
an inert mound of variegated feathers,
face down, beak between the boards.

Fix my gaze on intricate pattern,
shapes and colors of its rigid feathers,
patches of black and white, yellow and gray,
never seen when finches feeding or in flight.

Gently invert bird with end of broomstick.
Eureka, it lives! Gasping, trembling,
scrawny legs pointing skyward,
dark beady eye stares me down.

Try to help the fallen flier recover
from headlong flight into unseen door.
Sudden flutter and whoosh of wings.
Kamikaze finch flies into rising sun.

Light Verse

We are
sifting lumens
in the black firmament,
changing masses of light into
shimmers.

The sun,
eclipsed anew,
glowers in heated rage
at the lifeless, impudent rock,
the moon.

Fire glow
attracts hikers
lost in deep forest night,
reassures, warms, gives promise
of life.

Beacons,
high on sea rocks,
guide panicky sailors
along hidden perilous shores
homeward.

The light
in her moist eyes
reflects the gratitude
in her heart. She knows for certain
he's back.

Messages from Beyond

The first snow of November
sprawled on the lawn's lap,
leaving, as it melted,
a pre-obliteration pattern
of alien writing. Cuneiform
messages from beyond
spelling out a fleeting reprieve
for history—pleas for succor,
bursts of advice.

Martin Luther to Pope Leo:
"Most blessed Father, I tire
of waiting for your response
to my ideas for the betterment
of the Church and have gone
on vacation to the Canary Islands."

Hannibal to his veterinarian:
"Please send advice by swiftest
messenger on the proper treatment
for panting and shivering elephants."

Godot to Estragon and Vladimir,
patiently waiting for him:
"Sorry. I have been delayed
by a series of avalanches and floods.
I will come when the roads clear."

To Marco Polo from his import
representative in Venice:
"Business is booming. Urgent
that you send second shipment
of spaghetti without delay."

Captain Robert F. Scott
to the Royal Geographical Society:
"Mea culpa. The Norse
were right. Please send skis
and sled dogs at once."

From Icarus, high above Crete:
"The sun, the sun . . .
beware of melting . . ."

But minutes later the messages
melt into a puny puddle, where,
addressees unknown, they languish
in the dead-letter box of history.

Oranges

Golden-hued spheroids, bumpy outer peel,
sumptuously fragrant, pale yellow inner skin,
moist, sensuously slippery to the hand,
mischievously resist peeling, invade
finger nails, juice oozes then cascades out
luring nose and tongue, bean-shaped
segments snuggle in close embrace,
cradle germs of next generation,
shocking sensation of sweet-sour
on tongue, antidote to scurvy,
common street tree of Seville,
treasured old-time Yuletide stocking
stuffer, hypnotic scent of tropics,
follow up to dreaded dose of castor oil.

Patio Dragon

Lichen-weathered, dog-like,
he rests on green haunches,
cerise talons clutching leaf-draped
garden bed mulch. Subtle smirk
belies intensity of blood red eyes,
nostrils blackened from spurts of fire.
Majestic in repose, patio dragon
guards, challenges, threatens.

Picture This Picture

Horizonbereft, five slender jars float
unfettered in their rectangular world.
Darkly transparent, blue like sapphires,
brown as coffee, forest-green hued,
they hold themselves erect, treelike.
In mutual fear of shattering contact,
they remain close but separate.

Gestures of homage or mockery,
inky outlines trespass over, under
and behind the bottle forms.
The spectral lines, rendered
with distortion, imply a hint
of the vagaries of hostile fate
or of trespass by sinister forces.

A few containers appear stationary
while others seem to be in motion,
both ascending and sinking.
With destinies intertwined,
in a flat, inflexible universe,
their freedom is illusory.

The artist watches with a knowing smile;
she relishes ensnarement of the beholder.

Puppet Head

Part man, half devil, balance vampire.
Horns rise from swinish ears, point forward,
hinting of serious intent, suppressed anger.
Wide-set eyes, inexplicably azure,
threaten beneath furry crimson eyebrows,
hair-covered nose. Mouth and chin jut
out flanked by oversized blood-hungry teeth.
Triangular face terminates in orange goatee.
Lion's mane of unkempt hair explodes
around glaring face, a halo of fire,
starkly warning, threatening.
But the hair, the hair is baby-bottom-soft,
silky, soothing, sensual to the touch,
refuting the presence of absolute evil.

Purple

Most majestic of colors, begotten
through coupling of red and blue,
signature look of royalty, power.
Worn by kings and bishops,
favorite of elderly ladies in particular,
flamboyant women in general.

First name of finches and grackles,
herons and martins, sandpipers and trilliums.
Descriptive of foxglove, fringed orchids,
violets, irises, rampaging loosestrife.
Indicator of unbridled language,
critical label for overblown prose.

Regal tone of grape jelly, Concord wine,
berries, elegant eggplant.
Souvenir of falls and bruises.
Heart-felt homage to the wounded.

Runcible Tune

J.S. Bach.
flatly weary
of double-stranded
fugues,

sharpened
his quill and noted
that a triple-pronged
melody,

two parts broad,
uplifting, a third
honed to counterpoint,
can resolve itself

into appetizing
harmony, baroque yet
functional—
a runcible tune.

Salt

Flavor of the sea,
name for experienced sailors,
neutralization offspring of acid and base,
savory provider of piquancy,
basic taste to the tongue,
preserver of meat,
melter of ice,
threat to heart and kidneys,
component of tears,
partial salary of Roman legions,
final structure of Lot's spouse.

Sawdust

invades everything,
under, around, between,
in the air, atop the blinds,
through the vents, into the closets.

Sawdust, redolent of bygone
butcher shops, their floors strewn
with remnants of slaughtered trees,
sucking up blood of bovine, fowl, swine.

Silken Cats

Silken are cats, warm and soft to feel,
cherish gentle abdominal strokes.

Abyssinian, Persian, Birman.

Furry bellies sensual to touch,
smooth as cashmere, velvet, angora.

Shorthair, Longhair, Balinese, Burmese.

Lithesome, sybaritic, full of grace,
move proudly, tails aloft like banners.

Save the poor *Manx*, no tail to tell.

Silver

Silver, baser than gold, still lovely to behold,
gleans in dark tresses, which often depresses.
Hue of quarters and dimes. Moonlight it mimes.
Voice of fine singer. His dulcet tones linger.

Soccer Teams

Red and green versus purple and gold
in full career, hellbent for leather
orb. Don shin-high socks and cleated soles.
Dribble with foot, ricochet with skull,
charge enemy space, penetrate box.
Run and attack, reverse and defend,
capture ball, intercept low passes,
pant and sweat. Elude cards of yellow,
eschew the red. Advance, plunge on. Goal!

Storm

Thunder
growls under
murky clouds.
Bolts of
lightning
electrify
agitated sky.
Pelting rain
impacts land.
Night, angry,
chastises heat
of summer day,
calls for
profound
penitence.

Tai Chi

Contemplative silence.

Arms lift, right fist shelters left thumb.
Arms rise to salute brow as body bends
from hips, hands seek ground. The bow.

Slow, slow motion.

Body unfolds like drowsy blossom.
Clasped hands greet heart, then forehead.
Arms waft down, yield to gravity.

Slow, slow motion.

Grasp the bird's tail.
White stork spreads wings.
Carry tiger to the mountain.

Slow, slow motion.

Arms shoulder height, outstretched,
palms face earth. Arms float down as knees
imperceptibly bend. Tai Chi commences.

Slow, slow motion.

Body turns to right, left leg straight, right bent
bearing weight. Right arm out, palm down, reaches
toward imagined foe. Left arm cocked, defends
torso.

Slow, slow motion.

Ward off monkey.
Move arms like clouds.

Part wild horse's mane.
Slow, slow motion.

Left foot advances to right, arms hold invisible ball.
Brief sitting motion, weight shifts forward to left leg,
Left arm curls in front of chest.

Slow, slow motion.

Wordlessly Tai Chi continues.
One hundred eight separate steps,
many repeated, others unique.

Slow, slow motion.

Fair lady works shuttles.
Step up to seven stars.
Draw bow to shoot tiger.

Slow, slow motion.

Ballet of knee bends, weight shifts, twists
around spine, turns, controlled kicks,
backward motions, forward lunges, arms reaching.

Slow, slow motion.

No extraneous thoughts.
Concentrate on body, stretching.
Flow with the universe.

Golden cock stands on one leg.
Creep low like snake.
Push needle to sea floor.

Slow, slow motion.
Contemplative silence.

Tank Fish

Bombarded by a stream of bubbles,
they pace in their watery prison,
sinuously turn, ascend, descend,
hover in a finite universe.

In this piscine paradise
(ample food, no predators)
they bemoan the lack of freedom,
their empty existence.

Three Peonies

Varying in color and age,
three fragrant peony bushes
reveal themselves.

The oldest, bridal-white, erect,
blossoms crowning luxuriant green,
exudes confidence.

The second, emphatically cerise,
vying to surpass the others
in primacy of blossom, floral abundance,
droops under its mass of flowers.

Diffidently light pink, the youngest one
modestly accepts its immature state
and shyly opens three perfect blossoms.

Twilight

Atop the rise, a lonely bench looks
into the long vista, meditating.
Snow falls, a scrim to trees and lakes,
blurs, then fades horizon firs.

Sky and slope meld in grays and whites,
divided by the diagonal hill.
A bedraggled squirrel waits,
perches on the seat, then vanishes.

A cardinal nestles, its vivid red
accenting the scene, then wings away.
An elderly woman, thin as a reed,
stares out her window, watches wane of day.

Twilight at Senior Housing, Ithaca, New York

Cool, clear evening, gentle sky.
In silence three deer saunter past,
sample greenery, evaporate into dark.
Lone lifeless tree, draped in feral
vines, stands at forest edge.
Two branches, shaped like a harp,
tower over nearby living trees.
As light ebbs, a raven maintains watch.

Uncoiled

Don't bother
with rattlesnake,
it's mostly bone.
Don't eat the rattle,
just leave it alone.
A gourmet offering,
a challenge to eat,
the fearsome creature
sautéed in defeat.

Verily

Delicate accents of yellow, pink, violet
lie nested within a spacious spectrum
of emergent greens. With leaden
abruptness they morph plant by plant
into a wallow of verdant sameness.

The flatulence of internal combustion
throttles the scent of vernal renewal
that once elated the crystalline air.
Lilting breezes stifle under layers
of humidity, curl in on themselves.

Sprightly gaits shuffle amid sadistic heat,
slog into torpor, succumb to malaise.
Mosquitoes and gnats by the thousands
descend to torment. Sodden garments
adhere leechlike to panting torsos.

Storms rage; power fails. Skin cancer
devours. The reek of suntan oil
bonds with that of greasy barbecue.
Tempers shorten. Crime proliferates.
Energy dribbles away. Hope aestivates.

Summer's acomin' in.

What Happens in the Night

Mysterious streams flow past dark distant forests.
Astral hosts streak through twilit skies.
Azure spirits ascend as spectral creatures
scurry to find hapless prey.
Windswept woodland fires rage and roar.
Ghostly rocket ships whoosh outbound
as faintly-perceptible forces vie for supremacy.
The unseen restless sea murmurs incessantly.

V. HUMOR

Baby Bruin

I loved the little red chair
that Papa worked like a bear
to design and build for me.
Now it's just a heap of
fire wood and splinters,
relics of an unbearable visit.

Baton

Eight faint notes, some of them A's,
down a gray baton cascade,
lazily play, gyrate unabated.
Overrated maestro won't deign to face
the great disgrace of his base pace.
Dismayed, he loses face—floored the chord.

Bun in the Oven

This is how I came to be,
my beginning, stirring, savory.
Begat by hunger,
expressed in the fervor of a merger—
warmed oil, powdery whiteness—
creating splendid blending,
one part inseparable from the other.

Nurturing fluid,
particles of my future self,
graced, embraced me.
I assumed a shape befitting
my protective holder. Dark
globular lumps draped my head,
gave me a crown, foretelling
what I would soon become.

People inquired, asked when
I would appear, solid but soft,
to be admired and desired.
Slowly I grew, developed,
became complete in the heat.
Gestation over, I emerged
to hurrahs of glee: *Gimme! Gimme!*
They call me Streuselkuchen.

Butter

Nothing beats the sight, the taste,
the subtle scent of God's gift
from cows—sleek, smooth,
delicious butter, yellow globs
that slowly melt and penetrate
steaming stacks of golden pancakes.

But, but

slather and enjoy it wantonly
on bread and steamed anything,
drop it with abandon into hot rum,
use it to sauté onions and peppers,
blend it into custards and pies.
In the end it becomes one big

butt, butt.

Geriatric Vacation

Alone at home, Joan wrote a poem.
In frayed beret, Ray played croquet.
Will, the shill, was ill, took a pill, then a spill.
Petty Betty ate spaghetti on the jetty.
Ida tried to hide a pie—not to lie.
Ruth, forsooth, chewed on her tooth,
   loothened it.

Go, Goat, Go

Nanny, you are a lady, it's udderly obvious.
Your gentle pink undercarriage sustains life,
provides friendly feta and its cousins.
I kid you not. Your wavy beard
and rearward curved tiara make you
seem so horny. I am in awe of the spring
of your agility and the scope of your appetite.
Trust me, kind omnivore, I promise never
to rile you, no butts about it.

Gold-Threaded Wide-Brimmed Hat

You'll recognize me by my floppy yellow hat,
wide-brimmed, high-crowned, threads of gold.
On my lap I'll hold my dear calico cat.
Approach me directly. I love men who are bold.

*Do I want to keep this strange blind date
in the only place that's prudent to meet,
just inside a cemetery's wrought iron gate?
I cannot! It is true. I've frozen feet.*

A Great Golden God

The temple throbbed with the excited
murmurs of the faithful as they entered
the sanctuary, its vaulted ceiling
aglow with azure light.
The males wore prescribed garb of black
and white. Swaths of cloth in various hues,
often agleam with iridescence,
partially covered the bodies
of the females. A huge statue
of the great gold god
dominated the altar.
Its metallic visage
displayed no discernible emotion.
The ceremony began. Lights flashed
on and off as mammoth moving images
cast themselves upon the wall facing
the congregation. Music played
intermittently. A succession of prelates
and virtual virgins took turns
approaching and departing
the high altar. They unfolded
with reverence small pieces of scripture
and upon reading the words exhorted
the assembled to waves of frenzy.
Chosen ones then emerged from the mass
of excited communicants to be embraced
by the priests and the virgins. Small
golden replicas of the idol were thrust
into their trembling hands. The selected
then fell into a trance, wherein they chanted
ritual phrases of gratitude to the temple,
to their beloved ones, and to a multitude
of their fellow worshippers. The rite
lasted for hours as each priest or virgin intoned
the sacred syllables . . . **and the winner is . . .**

Group Therapy

Eleven college people, prof, undergrad, alums,
sit in the writing workshop on educated bums.
As a catalyst to unleash their literary jewels,
they draw childish pictures like a pack of fools.
In vain they attempt to write words that are snappy.
The bottom line is that it keeps them quite happy.

Host

Up and down the Mediterranean coast
Don Giovanni was the greatest host.
His parties started with an outrageous toast
and always served a gigantic roast.
Of hubris the glib roué had the most
till visited by a stone-faced ghost,
who terminated the Don's wanton boast
that he had every woman from pillar to post.

If I Could Transform the World, I'd

turn the Red Sea into molten chocolate,
allow the Egyptian host to go down with a smile,

let Jesus hop off the cross laughing
that it was only a practical joke,

make the whale become a vegetarian
and expectorate Jonah in disgust,

stir priests and rabbis, ayatollahs and lamas
in a blender, create a universal creed,

reverse global warming and all pollution,
erase greed and hate and revolution.

Laura Doubting

Committed to being a math major, I now have major doubts. My Doberman, three spaniels, two huskies and six randomly-sized dachshunds are the true focus of my existence. Everything I do and ponder equates with my love, no my adoration, for my canine friends. Their presence adds up to the total rationale for my life, helps me subtract worries and disappointments, multiply moments of fulfillment, chart the origin of my undivided devotion to them. I cannot calculate being without my countless companions. They compensate to the nth degree for the infinite dreariness of my circle of family and acquaintances. Whenever they approach me in their array of wagering appendages, my heart soars exponentially.

Yes, yes, goodbye math. I am off to vet school.

Lewis Carroll Weds
Walt Whitman

I see jabberwockies swinging, their many mimsies I see,
Those of toves, each of them swinging, vorpalling, beamish and free,
The pentercar swinging as he gimbles his flank or fork,
The mason jarring as he outgrabes his tumtum or swings off his cork,
The manboat swinging on what trumbles his float,
The handdeck swinging o'er the frumious moat,
The makershoe swinging as he splits his gyre,
The bankersnatch setting his second big fire,
The cutterwood's swing, the boyplow lost in the bath,
His gimbledink lies in the borogoves of wrath,
The uffish swinging of the snickersnack or of the youngish tife,
Or of the slithy jubjub brilliging for its fife,
All swinging as it pleases themselves or none,
The day honors the wabe and then it's done,
At night the herd of young whifflers, galumping and moming,
Swinging with open maws like pigeons homing.

Literary Idol

I'd love to meet Billy Collins,
my favorite American writer,
whose insight and poems
inspire and delight.

We'd dine in my choice of restaurant,
with his selection of wine.
Between shrimp cocktail and
bouillabaisse, we'd chat about
the building blocks, style,
and thoughts informing his writing.

Over chocolate fudge cake ala mode
and coffee (his black and real, mine
decaf and light) we'd joke and rhyme
and share our poems till late at night—
then jostle over who pays the check.

Loveless Museum Image

My emotions and brain are moved
by a trio of Renaissance figures,
a dour male flanked by two unhappy women,
faces full of anger, disappointment, resentment.

With obvious reluctance,
they touch each other,
feel the rise and boil of bile.

"I'll never marry this foppish man."
"My son is much too good for you."
"Mother, not her. It's Harold I desire."

Miser

A girl should always fear a miser,
who makes her pay for what he buys her,
who in his apartment hugs then ties her.
Afterwards she's so much wiser.

Mythology

I didn't myth you at all
declared Myth Melitha
to her main man as he hurled
mythlaid Madras material
at his mythress. The mythmatched
lovers mytheriously meandered
between mythunderstandings
and mutual mythery.

A myth is as good as a mile.

Obesity

Not fat, not chubby, just right-on zaftig.
Like, I'm sixteen, one cool chick,
blue eyes, long lashes, curly hair,
and a bod well-stacked, full, sexy.
My rolling curves, you know,
all smooth softness, invite boys
to caress and cuddle. No bony
angles or hint of anorexic stuff.

My rosy roundness, irresistible,
alluring, grows on you like
brownies a la mode, double
cheeseburgers, crispy super
fries, hot fudge sundaes,
strawberry cheesecake.
Rubens would have adored me.

Pillage

Perfumed by mixed metaphors
and the scent of adventure,
I waft away from my sleeping self,
take an exotic trip, float to strange
cities, visit alien nations. Free
of wearisome, snuffling protoplasm,
unburdened by baggage, I select
as my transport the flow of time
in the eye of space.

The first destination is the port of Lisinopril,
suffused with serenity and lust for malaise.
I go on to Lipitor to wallow in virtual feasts
of butter and beef, cream and caviar.
In a visit to Lanoxin I dance the universe
away to a slow and steady beat.

Then Mount Premarin seduces me
and I flee the lethargic heat of Atenolol.
During a sojourn in Glucosamine,
by the border with Chondroitin,
I achieve a painless victory
in the local double triathlon.

The opera festival in Coumadin
is my final stop. What a disappointment.
The voices are thin, the characters bloodless.
I head homeward to hover over
and try to reenter my slumbering body,
but the imprint of its former presence
on the sheet has cooled down, flattened out.

Quite a Day

You think you had a rough day!

First I spied a nervous rabbit,
really hung up on punctuality,
nattily attired but lacking gloves and fan,
scampered away mumbling about a duchess.

Hungry, I snacked on some cake
and a bit of mushroom,
sipped from a smallish flask.
Size of my world went beserk,
shrinking and expanding.

Met unstable grinning feline,
full of gossip, lacking physical focus.
Played round of croquet using
feathery pink mallet and spiny ball
with mind of its own.

Attended world's worst tea party:
unruly guests, lousy food.
Later riddled with questions
by caterpillar with nicotine habit.

Called as witness at trial of bakery
thief, then attacked by entire court.
Narrowly escaped axe of neurotic local ruler,
serious proponent of death penalty.

So how was your day?

Retirement

Retirement is hell and not a pleasure.
No time for rocking chair nor leisure.

Calendar tyranny every day
erodes the freedom to relax or play.

Monday tai chi, Spanish, feed the birds.
Tuesday poetry, art and words.

Wednesday tai chi, some racquetball.
Thursday walking, talking, go to mall.

Friday read to kids, index the Journal.
Saturday more activity eternal.

Sunday study, write a poem,
grateful to be staying home.

Interspersed on my dance card
are shopping, cooking, cleaning hard,

theatre, music, movies too,
hardly time to e-mail you,

restaurants, reading, gardening plans,
feed the cats, fill their pans,

concerts, TV, reading of plays.
The pace consumes all my days.

Please ignore my complaining voice.
This all happens by my choice.

Stone from Hell

Satan left a smooth, seductive stone
upon my mother's kitchen stove.
Marveling at its gleaming beauty,
black adorned with writhing scarlet fish,
she picked it up then loudly screamed.
It burned her hand, shot bolts
of pain through palm and arm.
Calling on her Old World lore,
she quickly set her silver pot aboil,
muttered ancient healing words, then
cooked the hell out of that damned rock.

What's New

When found by the frantic crew,
lying under a tarp behind the zoo,
all that remained was his left shoe.
He had gone to meet his fourth wife Sue,
who was an angry renegade Jew.
She hid her bills until past due,
a habit which she wouldn't eschew.
He complained till his face turned blue
and threatened a divorce or two.
To where he is, there's till no clue.
She did him in, I'm sure it's true.
But that's a tale of another hue.

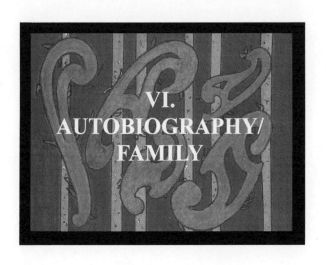

VI. AUTOBIOGRAPHY/FAMILY

Almost, Almost

A profusion of mauve-pink buds
on my cherished rose of Sharon bush
almost, almost made their long-awaited debut
before the herd of deer devoured them.

On the eve of a long-planned visit
to a friend in the Midwest,
I heard my father's final words,
a call for his nitroglycerine tablets.
I almost, almost made that trip.

The top ten students out of 300
in the high school graduation class
sat on the stage to receive all manner
of academic honors. Number eleven,
I almost, almost joined them.

I nurtured willowy late-blooming
magenta cosmos well into October.
They almost, almost achieved
flowering before a sudden storm
struck and demolished them.

I also planted giant marigolds
to accent my autumn flower beds.
They almost, almost lived to flaunt
their golden orange when
a cold front frosted them black.

I almost, almost believe that either
an inexplicable cosmic force
or a vengeful deity tries to thwart
everything I want and love.

Beloved Grandson

It hurt us to see you so upset,
angry that a stranger questioned
your honesty, your intentions.
In addition, we compounded
your dismay by lecturing you
on the appearance of wrongdoing
despite your intrinsic innocence.

We are sorry we jumped on you
when you anticipated solace.
In our rush to protect and teach you,
we denied you compassion and comfort.

Please try to understand.
We do love you dearly and want
to keep you from harm. Forgive us.
We embrace you unconditionally.

Clench

My jaw clenching is an ocean wave.
It ebbs, relaxes, regroups its forces,
then rears itself up, regains strength,
crests, and roars back, a tsunami
crashing jaw against jaw.
The pain! The ecstasy! The urge to repeat!

Why pursue this self-destruction?
Why impel tooth against tooth?
Irrational fear and stress
compel me to clench again and again.

If my husband is late coming home, did he succumb?
If he dies before me, how will I go on?
How can I cope with upkeep of the house
or the mystery of family finances?
Does my erratic pulse portend a stroke or debilitation?
What will be my legacy?
What will become of my paintings and my poems?
Will they mark me as a second-rate dilettante?

I may laugh and joke on the outside, but
the clench grinds on.

Closing Moment

The bride and groom were Jewish,
practiced no religion at all.
He invited a judge from work
to officiate at their civil wedding,
which duly moved through phrases
ordained by the State of New Jersey.

At the closing moment of the ceremony,
the judge asked the quasi-newlyweds
to repeat the traditional vow promising
to love, nurture, cherish unto death.
The bride echoed the familiar words until
she heard: *In the name of the Father* . . .

Complete silence, followed by
an interminable pause.
The small wedding assemblage
awaited her response. Was this
a civil ceremony, free of religion?
The groom's face stiffened with concern;
he feared embarrassing the judge.
The parlor clock ticked mercilessly.

In a semi-quavering voice, the bride
murmured: *In the name of the Father* . . .
The ceremony continued apace until
the nuptial pair invoked each
member of the Holy Trinity.
In retrospect, it did no great harm
to garner extra blessings. The marriage
soon enters its fifth decade.

Cutting Back

Spring.
Grass and weeds
race ahead of me,
assault with outrageous vigor
my dozen garden beds.
By the thousands,
intrusive green blades
bayonet their way
among irises, peonies,
daffodils, capture
the places reserved
for annuals.

The rampage of lust
for vernal succession
rends me between desire
and reality. Time devours
my stamina, my ability,
beset by enervating heat
and winged blood seekers,
to continue to garden
at my accustomed pace.
I face the need to downsize,
to concede to the invaders
the most overrun plots.
Daunted, I dare not desist.
And next spring?

Dark Encounter

The deer fell out of the blackness
onto the hood of our car.
I watched the creature ricochet
off into nowhere.
The metal of the car convulsed,
heaved, and raised mountains,
pieces spewing into the night.

Dear Greg Lardner,

you bastard! How could you take advantage
of my naivete and loneliness! Relaxing
from the stress of preparing for a new
career, I was walking along Sixth Avenue
heading for the greenery of Central Park.
You accosted me, asked directions to Roseland,
then suggested going for a drink.

How I loved your articulate speech, Canadian-accented,
and the sparkle of your eyes. You were so amiable,
self-possessed, intelligent, laughed at my quips,
told me I had character. You took me to elegant
restaurants, introduced me to artichokes, caviar,
and fine wine. Your little red Karman Ghia filled
me with anticipation. "A bachelor's car"
you called it. Naturally, I thought.

Weekdays we picnicked on Fire Island,
attended concerts and plays, took long walks
on Riverside Drive. You gave me your work
number but never your home phone or address.
You had "business obligations and paperwork"
to do on weekends. Puzzled, I wanted to believe
and swallowed your tale. My friends guessed
you might be married but when I challenged you,
you claimed bachelorhood. With faith
born of desperation, I believed. I believed.

Then work took you to Europe. Postcards greeted
me from Germany, France, and England as
the weeks without you stretched on. Fate, defying

statistics, brought us together one Sunday
afternoon on Fifth Avenue. I saw you coming
toward me, hand in hand with a short dark woman,
wearing a huge diamond ring, and with a young
girl in tow.

Shocked, I let you pass and then ran after you.
"I thought you were in Europe!" You turned
actor, responded as though you had met me
somewhere but forgot my name. You
introduced your wife and daughter, then strolled
on. Stunned, I stood wordless. I wanted to cry out
that we had been seeing each other for months
on more than a hand-holding basis. Compassion
for your wife and child bought my silence.

Greg, you shit, I really cared for you. Forty years
later your callous betrayal of me and your wife
still fills me with chagrin and humiliation.
How could I have been so foolish, so trusting?
Just once more I long to be with you in the dark,
in a subway station on the local track.
I want to stand right behind you
as the express train roars and rattles by.

Best regards.

Divorce

We lived quietly, no endearment, hugs,
kisses. Father, humorless, stoic,
seldom argued, kept conversation brief.
Mother remained home, shopped,
played mahjong, attended charity meetings.
Dad worked hard, six long days a week.

On Sundays the routine changed.
We dressed up, went to a restaurant,
saw a movie, ate a simple supper,
listened to the radio, went to bed early.

One day, in Dad's presence, Mom bemoaned
the boredom of her daily existence.
I asked why they didn't get a divorce.
Angry responses exploded around me.
I was never to mention the subject again.

What was amiss in our family? I never found out.
The routines ground on. The boredom endured.
In his forty-ninth year angina killed my father.

Doors

June 13, 1964. An elevator door opens
to animated conversation and laughter.
A woman wearing a pale blue dress
with corsage of white roses and carnations
steps out. She has an elaborate hairdo
and light makeup, a glint of gold on her hand.
A man follows clad in a dark blue suit,
light blue silk tie and white boutonniere.
Grains of rice tumble from their heads,
leaving a white trail to apartment 1017.
They open the door and close it behind them.

Dream Colors

1.

Starless night at ocean side
high tide, wild surf,
roll after towering roll,
dark waves disintegrating
into white froth atop
sinister black water.
I ride an enormous breaker
as it curls and surges shoreward.
Filled with dread and fragile
exhilaration, I remain above
the tons of roiling water, ride
in triumph to the somber sand.

2.

I spy a large short-haired cat,
perched on the lap of an unknown person.
No ordinary feline, she is boldly calicoed
with big, irregular splotches of white,
black, burnt sienna and intense turquoise.
My artist's eye is ecstatic. Where can I
obtain such a magnificent cat?

3.

My neighbor's tall, handsome, white-
moustached husband and I stand outside
his apartment door, contemplate
the pleasure of the unthinkable,
anticipate the afterglow of its guilt,
reluctantly decide to go for it.

Ecce Homo!

My husband is a clever, no, a brilliant man,
who mastered the mystery of physical chemistry,
became a formidable player of chess, immerses
himself in music, theatre, and art. He is a liberal
advocate of global peace and justice. His manhood
was affirmed by prowess in squash and skiing
and the siring of three children. He has the touch
of a wizard in repairing or building almost anything.
But by the dawn's early light, this regal
Renaissance man becomes the king of crabs.

Elegy

I wish to talk to my dead father
whose untimely passing warped my life.
(Nineteen was too young for such a blow.)

Over sixty years I've dwelt in dread
of sudden loss of friends and lovers.
In forty years of marriage I've feared
widowhood, abject abandonment.

I'm sorry I couldn't save you, Dad.
You were born too soon and died so young.

Exchange

Let me keep my fact-filled mind,
knowledge garnered and honed
over eight decades of living.

Magnanimously I offer my time-worn
body in exchange for the callow one
I had at age twenty. Let me pour all
the wisdom and experience of a lifetime
into that fresh, vigorous shell.

Such a monstrous waste
to relinquish to eternal dust
my treasured store
of skills and knowledge.

I defy the human condition!

Floral Echo

I have abandoned my flowers,
left them alone to survive
summer's incursion of grass
plus other pernicious invaders.

Eighteen years I tended the garden,
watered and weeded and fertilized.
I enter my final quarter century,
wearied by the many years.

I've lost all gardening stamina,
use my meager energy to husband
my husband, look after him,
as he recovers, with pace of snails,
a cerebral stroke survivor.

The Garden

My garden enslaves me every spring.
Geese return, snow cover thaws.
The tangled, overgrown thing
beckons, lures with weedy claws.

"Clean me, feed me, remove the mass
that inadvertently mulched my beds.
Repel the greedy encroaching grass.
Fill me with pinks and blues and reds."

Fighting bugs and deer, drought and heat,
I tend the garden every day.
My hour of energy I cannot repeat,
as I dig and sow, weed and spray.

Guilt

Longevity begets a heart of guilt
regretting words and acts unsaid, undone.
Bouquets of yearning lovers left to wilt,
abandoned friends and gratitude unwon,
the cries for help to light their dark ignored.
My life too full to please another soul.
Unheeded hands outstretched in hope, abhorred,
despised by me their supplicating role.
Forgive me, sister, mother, cousins, aunt,
my coldness, failure, lack of warmth and cheer.
You seek my love overtly given. I can't.
My old withdrawal marks profoundest fear.
    I want to change, to die in your embrace,
    be kind, engage, rejoin the human race.

Heat

Sagging and sweating, I try
to survive the steaming,
the roasting of this torrid
humid summer. Why is October
dragging its golden feet?

To my sweltering soul
the fall is a blessing,
winds of winter, paradise,
snow and rime, nirvana.

I try to keep my cool,
put my complaints on ice.
Breathless, I hold the door ajar,
await the advent of autumn.

Hypochondria

Why in the night do I think I am dying?
Why does vertigo stalk each twist and turn?
Why does marauding gas bayonet my gut?
Does back pain mean renal failure?
Does sudden headache portend stroke?
Does coughing predict consumption?
Do itchy lumps herald the curse of cancer?
Do sinister floaters threaten my vision?
Do I think I will survive until morning?

I Twirl a Mirror

Leafed canopy rotates
patterns of dappled green, brown,
affronts the eyes, alarms the brain.
Gorge rises, balance fractures,
waves of relentless motion
shrink the world,
imprison the vision,
inspire desire for stasis.

Kosher

My only daughter, an old maid of thirty-five,
visits me. Good-looking, clever, funny—
a jewel of many facets. Why no gold ring?

Mom, I've met a great guy. It looks serious.
Thanks, O Lord, that I live to hear this.
Birds start to sing, the sun outgleams itself.

I try to look calm as chicken soup. Oy vay,
then an awful thought dims the sun, stills birds
in mid note, chills the soup. Dare I risk

her wrath? Heavy like a matzoh ball, fear
presses on my heart. I must find out. I tremble
as I ask, "Maybe he is Jewish?" A reluctant *Yes.*

Praise to God. Birds and sun carry on
their celebration. My heart fizzes up like
an egg cream. Overjoyed, I sigh and inquire

what his name might be. Flat like a latke comes
her response, *Ronald North.* Mazeltov,
wonderful! It doesn't sound Jewish at all!

Listen to Your Body

My body possesses many a talking part.
Daily I speak to its weirdly beating heart.
By night I engage the acid-spewing gut,
entreat it to keep its factory shut.
At breakfast I address the arthritis in my back,
plead to let me ambulate on track.
Between midnight and the hour of four
I implore my sleepless brain to lock its door.
As you can see, I openly confess
my body is an unspeakable mess.

The Mason

The object of father's true pride,
elk tooth hanging from watch chain,
bolstered low self-esteem, clue
to meek, unschooled butcher's life.
Six days each week toiled
to sustain two kids and wife,
dreamt of career anew as surgeon,
not slicer of pork and beef.
Other accomplishments were few,
but be an Elk, a mason, what a coup!

My Atrial Fibrillation

AF, engendered by stress,
physical work, heat, humidity,
brooding over personal conflicts,
hours trekking marbled museum floors.

Strikes without warning, abruptly
crashes into my night's slumber.
I sense pounding in the chest,
feel the heart frantically trying
to escape its confining cage.

Waves of dismay, fear, weakness.
I lie clammy, rigid, too weary
to raise an arm, sit up, or walk.
In the dark I will the fearsome
beating to abate of its own accord.

Reach for "emergency" pills,
which will quell the wild thumping
but leave me exhausted for hours,
prisoner of my own body, fearing
the sadistic monster within will
resume its demonic rhythm.

Not Yet

In my eighth decade with most
of the necessary parts still
chugging along, missing nary a beat.
I think, I plan, I create, I appreciate, I jest,
I exercise, I organize, I bicker, I love.

I do lack a Nobel Prize, an Oscar,
an appointment as Poet Laureate,
a Pulitzer Prize, a solo show
in the National Gallery of Art,
a command performance as a
stand-up comic at the United Nations.
Thus I seek an outstanding legacy,
a painting, a poem, even a great recipe.

I am not ready for oblivion
or the great beyond, nor
do I have any immediate plans
to buy a farm. With a modicum
of luck, I do not intend to kick
a bucket within the next twenty years.
Whatever my number may be,
I do not concede that it will soon
be up. Pass over to the other side?
Sorry, I have no interest in rushing
wherever it is. Go to meet my maker,
whoever that may be? Strictly speaking,
my maker is the gametes of my mother
and father. But if I am to encounter them,
I choose to greet my parents in their entirety.

Death, meeting you is seldom nice.
Therefore, put thy sting on ice.

Pop's House

171 Ridgewood Avenue.
Ramshackle three-flat building
separated from look-alike neighbors
by sun-bereft sliver of alley.
Oaken icebox on Pop's back landing
continually drip dripped,
ravenous coal furnace nurtured
by grandchildren, ancient player
piano spookily produced music,
overhead toilet tank roared
whenever tail pulled.

Progeny

My children are watercolors,
shaped in my image, born of my style.
Wild at birth, these creatures
reflect transient fires,
yearn to be nourished,
cajoled into harmony.

Psychotherapist

I didn't know I was so angry
until I saw the therapist
who dug up decades of rage
phantom feelings of injustice
insidious low self-esteem
gargoyles of hidden guilt.

The Tale of the Manx

A brazen wanderer,
caudally challenged,
gender unknown,
handsome white body,
brindled stripes,
patrolled the perimeter
of our garden and lawn
ascended deck stairs,
peered through double glass
doors, outraged both our cats.

We planned to spray
the stairs to the deck
with semi-toxic repellent;
never got around to it.
Driving towards town
the day before yesterday,
I discovered the manx,
relaxed, stretched out
atop the yellow line,
a rural traffic victim.

Our problem resolved,
the trespasser gone,
we mourn its proud face,
feral audacity.

The Thing About You Is

that you created me, then proceeded,
however unintentionally, to destroy me.
You blamed me for your difficult delivery,
told me, "You almost killed me."

But I was totally innocent, the hapless result
of your careless behavior, neglect of medical
advice, inordinate fear of the process
of liberating me from your body.

You unabashedly craved overt affection
to the extent that I cringed and withdrew
from your every frantic embrace.
I was too angry to love you.

Alien to my sensibility, you burdened
me with feelings of inadequacy
and disappointment that I fell short
of your vision of a cuddly, pink daughter.

You laid on me your Old-World
values and superstitions, taught me
to fear "the other" and to cling
desperately to "our own."

At 27, I sought my own apartment,
and you bewailed the disgrace to the family,
deprecation of the quality of our home,
and my setting myself up as a prostitute.

Two Realms

My favorite realm is my painting studio,
high-ceilinged, double-glass-doored.
It houses dozens of CD's to embrace
the ears while eager hands and eyes revel
in ecstatic chromatic collusion.

I also favor a more sensual realm,
suffused with scent of lavender and rose.
Amid steamy dampness, I anticipate
the sound of rushing water beating
on tile and glass and await the velvet froth
of shampoo on my hands before I caress
myself with foaming perfumed bar.

Uncertainty

I could levitate, rise and float
two feet above the sidewalk,
body surfing in the air.
I feel uncertain that it was a dream.

Under My Influence

nothing has ever changed
either for the better or for the worse.
My spouse still gets grumpy
when I tell jokes before breakfast.
The cat still throws up on the carpet.
Our neighbors still believe in angels.
The ERA remains a still-born dream.
Most chefs still overcook the sprouts.
People are still greedy and inhumane.
The world still awaits the coming of peace.

What a Dish!

Food, food, snack, snack, eat, eat.
It's a compulsion I cannot beat.
I crave them all, vegetable and meat,
candy, soup, fruit, rice and wheat.
I worship chocolate as you know.
Ingesting it makes my psyche glow.
To my weight and heart it's a foe,
but I keep devouring as down I go.

What Matters

Fire! The house is burning!
Flames, smoke, heat, screaming alarms, panic!
Adrenaline pumping full bore. 9-1-1 called.
Scurry to rescue important things.
What matters?

The old man matters. Good husbands
hard to come by and this one honed
to near perfection after forty years.
Tear him away from computer,
push wallet, purse, keys, emergency
number list into startled hands.
Shuffle him out the front door.
"Get the cars out! I'll get the cats."

Cats matter. Probably spooked
from noise and smoke. Scatter
and hunker down in secret lairs.
No response to calling of names?
Dash about moribund house,
a Groucho Marx proffering
open can of tuna, irresistible lure.
Got them and multiple scratches.
Cats can apologize in the morning.

What else matters as swirling smoke
threatens from ceiling downward?
Our medications, my notebook of poems,
my lungs. Escape into fresh air.

All other things dispensable, replaceable.
Life matters. Creativity matters. Renewal matters.

When I Wrote About

the guilt in which I now wallow
and its effect on the hapless victim
of my self-centeredness, I did it
as an intellectual exercise, void
of emotion or personal responsibility.
I felt I was merely reciting some facts,
detached from any connection of one
human being to another, who loved
me and was reaching out to me.
We had the same parents, grew up
in the same environment,
but how different we were!

Who Was To Blame?

A somber gray scrim covers my childhood memories, pale translucent gray of windblown fog and denser slate gray of clouds that herald summer storms. Decades later isolated incidents and feeling rise from the mists, come into sharper focus.

I remain bereft of happy recollection of family affection, easy laughter, playfulness, overt joy. I recall the many privileges proffered my younger brother based solely on his gender. Clumsy, hirsute, acne-plagued, I was essentially friendless. I avoided my peers, feeling they would reject me out of hand. I suffered from ineptitude in dancing, singing, social graces. Angry at being female, I resented the pain, mess and odor of menstruation.

Random childhood memories continue to emerge through breaks in the grayness of the past. During my only stay at summer camp, at age eight, I had to undergo a nude health exam by a male physician. He spread apart my innocent legs and peered at my most private part.

When I was a twelve year old Hebrew school pupil, the building custodian attempted to fondle my pre-adolescent breasts. Betrayal and confusion compounded my fright when I later saw the molester talking and joking with the much-beloved and revered rabbi.

Another childhood incident concerned the inexplicable disappearance of my treasured penknife. I thought I had carelessly lost it. Decades later Mother confessed that she secretly purloined the knife because she deemed it dangerous and—especially for a girl—inappropriate.

During that summer away at camp, my mother abruptly stopped coming to see me. They told me that she was "visiting in Boston." Campers and counselors alike knew she was hospitalized, undergoing surgery. I had to deal with my mother's lack of confidence in me to handle the truth and with the conspiracy of the others to live her lie.

In my teen years I was unable to prevent my father's sudden death. I failed to find his nitroglycerine pills as he called for them.

Sixty years later my childhood memories persist as unhappy, painful moments to be endured but never outlived.

Who was to blame? Who was to blame?

Other Book By This Author:

"Explosion of Dragons"
© 2007
ISBN: 978-1-60402-965-9

Made in the USA